ADDICTED
to E-Cigarettes and Vaping

Carla Mooney

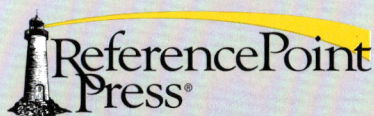

ReferencePoint
Press®

San Diego, CA

© 2020 ReferencePoint Press, Inc.
Printed in the United States

For more information, contact:
ReferencePoint Press, Inc.
PO Box 27779
San Diego, CA 92198
www.ReferencePointPress.com

LIBRARY OF CONGRESS CATALOGING-IN-PUBLICATION DATA

Name: Mooney, Carla, 1970– author.
Title: Addicted to E-Cigarettes and Vaping/by Carla Mooney.
Description: San Diego, CA: ReferencePoint Press, [2019] | Series: Addicted
   | Includes bibliographical references and index. | Audience: Grade 9 to
   12. |
Identifiers: LCCN 2019011288 (print) | LCCN 2019021871 (ebook) | ISBN
   9781682825686 (eBook) | ISBN 9781682825679 (hardback)
Subjects: LCSH: Vaping—Juvenile literature. | Smoking—Juvenile literature.
Classification: LCC HV5748 (ebook) | LCC HV5748 .M66 2019 (print) | DDC
   362.29/6—dc23
LC record available at https://lccn.loc.gov/2019011288

Contents

A New Epidemic

In December 2018 US surgeon general Jerome Adams issued a warning about a dangerous new trend sweeping the country: e-cigarettes and vaping. Adams warned that vaping, and teen vaping in particular, had become a significant public health threat. "It's why, today, I'm issuing just the fourth Surgeon General's advisory in over 10 years," Adams said. "There is an epidemic of use of e-cigarettes."[1] He was referring to the concerning results of several surveys that have found teens using e-cigarettes and vaping products in record numbers. The Food and Drug Administration's 2018 National Youth Tobacco Survey, for example, revealed that the number of high schoolers using e-cigarettes and vaping products increased 78 percent between 2017 and 2018. The increase in use is not limited to high school youth; the survey also reported that the number of middle schoolers using e-cigarettes increased 48 percent from 2017 to 2018.

A New Nicotine Device

E-cigarettes arrived on the US market during the middle of the first decade of the 2000s. Widespread advertising via television commercials, print advertisements, Internet ads, and social media made the devices appear cool and exciting, as did the celebrities who were photographed using them. Initially, e-cigarettes and other vaping devices were presented as healthier alternatives to traditional tobacco smoking. Unlike tobacco cigarettes, e-cigarettes have no tar, a sticky brown substance linked to throat and lung cancer. Neither do e-cigarettes contain many of the other cancer-causing chemicals found in tobacco cigarettes.

But just because e-cigarettes contain fewer or different chemicals than regular cigarettes does not mean they are safe. E-cigarettes still contain nicotine, the addictive drug in tobacco. In some cases, e-cigarettes and vaping products deliver even more nicotine to users than do regular cigarettes. Nicotine is highly addictive and is especially dangerous for developing teen brains. "We must take aggressive steps to protect our children from these highly potent products that risk exposing a new generation of young people to nicotine. Nicotine is uniquely harmful to young and developing brains [and] can cause learning, attention and memory problems, and it can prime the brain for addiction in the future,"[2] said Adams.

In addition, the aerosol produced by e-cigarettes and its flavorings can contain a variety of chemicals, such as propylene glycol, benzene, formaldehyde, and diethylene glycol. Some of these chemicals are known to be toxic or to cause cancer. However, because these devices are so new, the long-term health effects of using e-cigarettes are still being determined.

A Dangerous Reversal in Public Health Gains

As a result of aggressive antismoking public health campaigns, adult smoking rates in the United States have declined over the years. According to a 2018 report by the Centers for Disease Control and Prevention (CDC), only 14 percent of American adults (34.3 million) smoked cigarettes in 2017; this is a decline of 67 percent since 1965, when 42.4 percent of American adults smoked cigarettes. "The declines we saw in 2017 for adult smoking are certainly unprecedented,"[3] says Brian King, a deputy director in the CDC's office on smoking and health. Youth smoking is also on the decline. According to the 2017 National Youth Tobacco Survey, a record low of 7.6 percent of high school students smoked tobacco cigarettes compared to 36.4 percent in 1997.

The decline in adult and youth smoking rates is an important public health achievement: tobacco use is the number-one cause of preventable disease, death, and disability in the United States.

Teen E-Cigarette Use Is Rapidly Growing

A national survey has revealed that 1.5 million more students used e-cigarettes in 2018 than in 2017. The increase among high school students during that one-year period was 78 percent, resulting in a total of 20.8% of high school students. The increase among middle school students was 48 percent, resulting in a total of 4.9% of middle school students. Public health officials and others say they are alarmed by the huge increase in e-cigarette use among US teenagers.

Teen E-Cigarette Use, 2017–2018

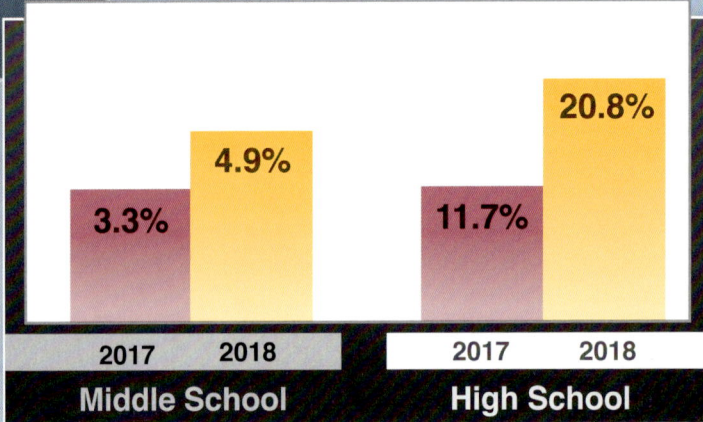

Middle School		High School	
2017	2018	2017	2018
3.3%	4.9%	11.7%	20.8%

Source: US Food and Drug Administration, "Youth Tobacco Use: Results from the National Youth Tobacco Survey," November 2018. www.fda.gov.

According to the CDC, more than 16 million Americans have at least one disease caused by smoking, and millions more are exposed to secondhand smoke. Smoking-related illnesses cost society more than $300 billion annually, which includes $170 billion in direct medical costs and more than $130 billion in lost productivity. Reducing the number of smokers improves health and reduces the economic costs of smoking-related illnesses. However, the arrival of e-cigarettes and vaping has started to reverse the progress made by antismoking campaigns. The 2018 National Youth Tobacco Survey showed that more than 3.6 million middle and high school students had used e-cigarettes in the past thirty days, which is a substantial increase of more than 1.5 million students. In other words, the number of teen e-cigarette users had more than doubled compared to the prior year. The report revealed that youth who are using e-cigarettes are vaping more frequently and are using flavored products more often than they had in the prior year. The sharp increase in e-cigarette use is driving an overall increase in youth tobacco product use as well. "[This is] a cause for grave concern," says CDC director Robert R. Redfield. "E-cigarette use is unsafe among youth, and it's critical that we implement proven strategies to protect our Nation's youth from this preventable health risk."[4]

> "All the work that happened, all the public health campaigns, the billions of dollars spent to try to eliminate tobacco use for kids has been undone."[5]
>
> —Jonathan Winickoff, a pediatrician at Massachusetts General Hospital in Boston

Millions Are Becoming Addicted

In a few short years, e-cigarettes have exploded in popularity, especially among teens. While smoking e-cigarettes may be safer than smoking tobacco, there are still serious risks. The ingredients "smoked" in these devices often pack a strong punch of nicotine, which is a highly addictive drug. They also contain dangerous cancer-causing chemicals. Although not everyone who vapes will become addicted, many will. "These products are really creating a resurgence," says Jonathan Winickoff, a pediatrician at Massachusetts General Hospital in Boston. "All the work that happened, all the public health campaigns, the billions of dollars spent to try to eliminate tobacco use for kids has been undone. Now we have millions of adolescents currently addicted to nicotine."[5]

Chapter One

The Smoke-Free Addiction

Nick English knew he had a problem with cigarettes, but he never realized trying to give up smoking would leave him addicted to vaping. He had started smoking as a social habit, and enjoyed having a few cigarettes on weekends with friends. By 2015, however, English was smoking several cigarettes per day, and even more when he was drinking. After a weekend of particularly heavy smoking, English's respiratory system paid the price: he would cough for a week and spit up huge globs of phlegm. Concerned for his health, he wanted to stop smoking—but he did not know how to do so. Then he saw a new commercial from the company Juul, which makes e-cigarettes. "Before I knew it, I'd ordered one for myself and fallen in love at first hit. Everything about the e-cigarette seemed, and felt, better than my old cancer sticks," he says. "The smell, the cost, the surprisingly strong amount of nicotine it delivered per hit. At the same social events where I once belched noxious, girlfriend-repelling, shirt-stinking tobacco fumes, I was now puffing crème brûlée-scented fog clouds."[6]

English never viewed e-cigarettes as entirely harmless, but he thought they had to be better for him than smoking traditional cigarettes. At first, vaping was almost too easy. He could vape anywhere, without having to go outside for a smoke break. The habit was simple to hide because the device looks like a computer flash drive and does not give off the telltale tobacco smell of traditional cigarettes.

Because vaping was so simple, English found himself doing it more and more; after a few years, he was vaping more often than he had ever smoked cigarettes. "My first e-cig had led to me vaping *all the . . . time*. All night when I'm out with friends and now all day while I'm at work," he says. English noticed that his e-cig never burned down

or "finished" the way a traditional cigarette did, making it difficult for him to regulate his consumption. "Maybe just one puff. Maybe one more. Like a never-ending pipe, you don't know when you've had enough, when you've had a cigarette's worth of nicotine. One quick puff to slay your stress can turn into one puff every few minutes, then whenever I get the slightest urge,"[7] he says.

Like many adults, English turned to e-cigarettes because he thought they were a healthier alternative to smoking. However, he soon found out that vaping had its own side effects. For one,

Many people start vaping because it is easier to hide than cigarette smoking. It doesn't smell bad, the device looks like a computer flash drive, and you do not have to go outside to do it.

his addiction to nicotine actually grew because of the high nicotine content of e-cigarettes. "Eventually, I was vaping pretty much all day, every day," he says. Vaping impacted his health in other ways too. "My lung capacity was absolutely destroyed. I couldn't do cardio to save my life; walking up stairs sucked the wind out of me," he says. "My stamina and day-to-day life was vastly more affected by this vaping habit than when I used to just smoke a few cigarettes on Saturday nights."[8] English's experience with e-cigarettes is common. Regardless of why they start vaping, many e-cigarette users find that their lives are quickly consumed by the tiny devices.

Exploding Vapes

In addition to the potentially harmful chemicals in their aerosol, e-cigarettes have other dangers. In rare cases, vaping devices can catch fire and explode. In 2018 the first vaping-related death occurred in Florida. The victim, Tallmadege D'Elia, was at home in St. Petersburg, Florida, when his vape pen exploded. D'Elia died from a projectile wound to the head. The explosion also started a fire in D'Elia's bedroom, where he was found with burns on about 80 percent of his body.

D'Elia was the first person to die from a vaping device, but many accidents have been reported. In 2017 the US Fire Administration reviewed 195 reports of fires and explosions related to e-cigarettes that occurred from 2009 to 2016. Many e-cigarettes (including Juuls) use lithium-ion batteries, which are more likely to explode. "No other consumer product places a battery with a known explosion hazard such as this in such close proximity to the human body," the administration said. "It is this intimate contact between the body and the battery that is most responsible for the severity of the injuries that have been seen. While the failure rate of the lithium-ion batteries is very small, the consequences of a failure, as we have seen, can be severe and life-altering for the consumer."

Quoted in Jacey Fortin, "This May Be a First: Exploding Vape Pen Kills a Florida Man," *New York Times*, May 16, 2018. www.nytimes.com.

Vaping Rises in Popularity

Since their introduction, e-cigarettes have skyrocketed in popularity. Approximately 10.8 million American adults currently use e-cigarettes, according to a 2018 study published in the *Annals of Internal Medicine*. The study also found that younger adults were more likely to use e-cigarettes, with more than half of users younger than age thirty-five.

E-cigarettes are popular because they are convenient, easy to use, and found everywhere. Users can readily buy vaping devices and pods, or cartridges, at gas stations and convenience stores. E-cigarette use is discreet and easy to hide because the devices often look like everyday objects, such as fountain pens or computer flash drives, and they do not leave behind the pungent smell of tobacco smoke.

E-cigarettes have become popular in part because many people believe they are a healthier alternative to smoking tobacco. Traditional cigarettes must be lit on fire and burned to produce smoke the user can inhale. Burning the tobacco produces tar, which is a substance that contains cancer-causing and other harmful chemicals. When the tobacco smoke is inhaled, the tar coats the inside of the throat and lungs, which can lead to cancer and other respiratory problems.

In contrast, e-cigarettes do not contain tobacco and do not burn any material. Instead, e-cigarettes release an aerosol that the user inhales. E-cigarettes are devices that typically include a mouthpiece, a cartridge that contains what the industry refers to as e-liquid, and a heating component fueled by a battery. The battery heats the e-liquid until it turns into an aerosol called a vapor. Vaping is the act of inhaling the aerosol into the lungs and exhaling.

Although many users believe that this aerosol, or vapor, is similar to a harmless water vapor, that is not the case. Like traditional cigarettes, e-cigarette aerosol contains nicotine, which is addictive. Additionally, the e-liquid and flavorings in e-cigarettes often contain a variety of potentially harmful chemicals and metals, including formaldehyde and lead. Also, the aerosols produced by e-cigarettes contain many fine chemicals and particles that have been linked to cancer, respiratory problems, and heart disease.

Teens Are Vaping in Record Numbers

Since the introduction of e-cigarettes, teens who have never smoked before have embraced them and are now vaping in record numbers. In a December 2018 survey by the National Institute on Drug Abuse (NIDA), 37 percent of high school seniors reported having tried vaping, an increase from 28 percent in 2017. Additionally, nearly 21 percent of seniors reported having vaped in the past thirty days, compared with 11 percent in 2017. The number of younger students vaping is also on the rise. The survey found increases in e-cigarette use for both eighth and tenth graders in 2018 as compared to 2017. "The most surprising news to me was how frequently teenagers are vaping," says Dr. Wilson Compton, NIDA's deputy director. "Right now over one-third of high school seniors report using a vaping product."[9]

Teens are often drawn to e-cigarettes because they are so easy to hide and use. Unlike cigarettes, vaping devices leave no burning tobacco smell to tip off teachers and parents. Instead, vaping produces a sweet-smelling cloud of vapor that disappears more quickly than regular smoke. The devices themselves are easy to slip into a pocket or purse. Often, parents and teachers do not know what to look for to determine whether a teen is vaping. "The vapor disappears quickly and it's masked by a scent such as mango, so you can't tell if it's someone's new lip gloss or candy," says Francis Thompson, the principal at Jonathan Law High School in Milford, Connecticut. As a result, teens are vaping at home, at school, and just about everywhere they go. At Thompson's school, staff noticed an increase in the number of students going to the bathroom and spending more time in there, often in groups. He sent teachers to investigate. "They were vaping,"[10] he says.

Teens are also drawn to the dizzying array of e-liquid flavors. Currently, there are about eight thousand flavors, many of which have appealing names such as Rainbow Candy and Glazed Donut. A study by researchers at the University of North Carolina School of Medicine found that fruity e-liquid flavors play a significant role in getting youth to try them. "The review shows that e-cigarette flavors appear to motivate e-cigarette and smoking initiation among youth," says Adam Goldstein, the director of the University of North Carolina Tobacco Intervention Programs and an author of the study. "The use of flavored e-cigarettes presents a dangerous gateway to nicotine addiction for youth."[11]

Leia Dyste, a nineteen-year-old at Northern Arizona University, is a typical teen who has embraced e-cigarettes. She took

> "The use of flavored e-cigarettes presents a dangerous gateway to nicotine addiction for youth."[11]
>
> —Adam Goldstein, the director of the University of North Carolina Tobacco Intervention Programs

Comparing Packs and Pods

Some types of e-cigarettes, like the Juul, use pods to deliver their e-liquids. A pod is a small container that holds about two milliliters of e-liquid. Users simply click the pod into their device and start vaping. Some pods are prefilled and disposable, but others are refillable. Each pod provides about two hundred puffs and the nicotine equivalent of twenty cigarettes, or about one pack.

However, unlike cigarettes, pods do not have a defined serving size. When smoking a traditional cigarette, users can easily measure when they start (when they light the cigarette) and when they finish (when it has burned to the filter and is no longer smokable). They can also count how many cigarettes they consume in a single day. In contrast, measuring the amount of e-liquid a person has used in a day is much more difficult. Users puff continuously, perhaps smoking less in one sitting than if they had smoked a traditional cigarette, but perhaps more throughout the day because of their continual use. It is the equivalent of snacking throughout the day rather than eating defined meals. Because it is very difficult to measure servings with a pod, it becomes very easy for users to consume more than they intend. For some casual users, a single pod might last for a week or more. Yet addicted users may find themselves going through a pod or more in a single day.

up vaping because she thought it would help relieve stress from school, and she was under the impression that e-cigarettes contained fewer carcinogens than tobacco cigarettes. On campus, Dyste is one of many teens who use e-cigarettes. She says that vaping has become a culture of sorts at school. "I think a lot of people feel left out if they don't have a vape to just pull out at any time, so that just kind of adds to the fact that it's such a new thing that everyone is doing,"[12] she says.

Juuling: Vaping's Hottest Trend

Among teens and young adults, one of the most popular vaping devices is made by the company Juul, which sells a small rectangular gadget that looks like a computer flash drive. A Juul's sleek design allows it to be easily hidden, making it especially popular with teens. "It's not uncommon for me to hit my Juul in bed, while doing homework and stuff like that,"[13] says a senior at Westfield High School in New Jersey. Another Westfield student says that she uses her Juul in school as a way to release stress. "If I get an opportunity to Juul in school, I take it. It's sometimes a nice feeling when I'm stressed out,"[14] she says. Whereas other vaping devices release clouds of scented vapor, a Juul releases short puffs of vapor that quickly disappear. Juul e-liquid also comes in several tempting flavors, including watermelon and mint. No matter the flavor, every Juul product contains a high dose of nicotine. In fact, a single pod holds about the same amount of nicotine as an entire pack of cigarettes.

Some teens, including nineteen-year-old Cassandra Cini, credit the company with making vaping increasingly popular with high school and college students. Cini, a sophomore at Keene State College in New Hampshire, describes Juul's appealing marketing campaign, which features brightly colored ads in which young people smoke with friends; the device is heavily advertised on popular social media sites. "It sounds cliché, but they made [vaping] seem cool," says Cini. "It just blew up almost like an Internet sensation."[15] Michael McCall, a twenty-seven-year-old at James Madison University, says vaping was rare on campus until Juul emerged. "No one was really into it until the Juuls came out,"[16] says McCall. According to the CDC, Juul e-cigarette sales increased from 2.2 million devices in 2016 to 16.2 million devices in 2017, an increase of 641 percent in a single year.

Growing Health Concerns

As more people use e-cigarettes, medical professionals are becoming concerned about the potential health consequences. Although long-term studies about the health effects of vaping are not yet available, a growing body of evidence indicates that the risks of vaping may outweigh any benefits.

From the beginning, e-cigarette makers have presented their products as healthier alternatives to smoking cigarettes. In fact, the landing page on Juul's website states, "Make the Switch: Juul was developed as a satisfying alternative to cigarettes."[17] According to the Food and Drug Administration (FDA), regular cigarettes contain more than ninety harmful or potentially harmful chemicals; e-cigarettes do not share many of their traditional counterparts' ingredients list.

Although vaping reduces a person's exposure to those ninety or so chemicals, vaping liquids often contain potentially harmful substances as well. Users might think they are just inhaling harmless vapor, but they are drawing a chemical-filled aerosol into their lungs. The particles in the vaping aerosol are so fine that they can slip past the lung's filtering system, sending them deeper into the lungs than smoke from traditional cigarettes. Many of these chemical particles have been linked to cancer, respiratory problems, and heart disease. "The e-cigarette industry has been trying to peddle that their products are safe, that they don't contain the nasty chemicals that you find in cigarettes," says Erika Sward, the assistant vice president of national advocacy for the American Lung Association. "As more and more research comes out, I think that we're not surprised to find that the e-cigarette industry has not been truthful and forthcoming about the chemicals that their products do contain."[18]

Some of the chemicals found in e-liquids and the vapors they produce include propylene glycol (used in antifreeze products), acetone (used in nail polish remover and paint thinner), formaldehyde (used as an embalming fluid), vegetable glycerin, and diacetyl, a chemical that has been linked to severe respiratory distress known as popcorn lung. Even though many of the additives in e-liquids have been approved by the FDA for eating, they have not been approved for heating and inhaling, which dramatically changes their chemical composition. When heated up by a vape pen or other device, these additives can produce formaldehyde and other toxic chemicals. They can also irritate and inflame the lungs, which can cause chronic bronchitis, scarring, and permanent lung damage. In some cases, the chemicals could begin to react with each other and form potentially toxic substances prior to heating, as soon as the e-liquid is mixed. "It's entirely possible that there may be tens or even potentially hundreds of compounds forming and we just don't know much about them,"[19] says Sven-Eric Jordt, a professor of anesthesiology, pharmacology, and cancer biology at Duke University School of Medicine.

A High Risk of Addiction

Even more concerning is that e-cigarettes contain significant amounts of nicotine, the highly addictive drug in tobacco. In fact, vaping e-liquids typically contain *more* nicotine than cigarettes. A single Juul pod is 5 percent nicotine, which is the equivalent of an entire pack of cigarettes. Although some users are unaware of the high level of nicotine, many others mistakenly believe that vaping is a safer way to consume nicotine. Regardless of how

Teenagers do not have fully developed brains. For this reason, teens who vape are more vulnerable than adults to nicotine addiction.

it is consumed, nicotine is highly addictive and can have harmful effects on health. For example, in pregnant women, nicotine threatens the developing fetus and can result in low birth weight, preterm delivery, and stillbirth. In adolescents, nicotine affects the brain and can impair memory, attention, and learning. Nicotine may also be linked to an increased risk of heart disease.

Teens who vape are likely to become addicted to nicotine faster than adults because their brains are still developing (until about age twenty-five). "The younger the developing brain is exposed to nicotine, the stronger and more rapid the addiction," explains pediatrician Jonathan Winickoff. "The earlier you become addicted, the harder it is to quit."[20] Winickoff warns that becoming addicted to nicotine as a teen can remodel the brain in ways that lower the addiction threshold for alcohol and other drugs, making kids more likely to abuse other substances later in life. In addition, teenage nicotine use can interfere with long-term cognitive functioning and increase one's risk of several mental and physical health problems in the future. Health experts like Dr. Christy Sadreameli, a spokeswoman for the American Lung Association, are concerned that e-cigarettes—and Juul products in particular—are creating a lifelong addiction for today's teens. "They've created an addiction that's going to be expensive," says Sadreameli. "It's much more likely to be a permanent thing, because teens [are] more likely to get addicted, in general. Using a very high-potency nicotine product during that vulnerable period of life—it's just a bad combination."[21]

Many teens may not even realize that e-cigarettes contain addictive nicotine. According to the antitobacco nonprofit group the Truth Initiative, 60 percent of teens mistakenly believe that vape

> "The younger the developing brain is exposed to nicotine, the stronger and more rapid the addiction. The earlier you become addicted, the harder it is to quit."[20]
>
> —Jonathan Winickoff, a pediatrician at Massachusetts General Hospital

products are largely just flavorings. In truth, nearly all e-cigarette products contain nicotine. Even teens who regularly use a Juul are slow to realize that their vaping habit has turned addictive. In a 2018 study of California high school students, teens reported using Juuls about twice as often as those who smoked cigarettes. "The youth who were using Juuls were using them more often," says senior researcher Bonnie Halpern-Felsher, a professor of pediatrics at the Stanford University School of Medicine. "They were using them a significantly greater number of days, which gives us a concern whether they are addicted to those products." At the same time, most of the teens said they did not feel addicted to the Juul. "When you asked them about their perceptions of addiction regarding these products, they didn't think they were addictive," says Halpern-Felsher. "There was a real disconnect between how they perceived these products and how their bodies are reacting to them."[22]

E-cigarettes have taken the world by storm. Users love the sleek gadgets and their sweet-smelling vapors. Yet many people are realizing that using e-cigarettes is far from a harmless habit. Although they do not burn tobacco, e-cigarettes still deliver nicotine, one of the world's most addictive drugs, along with several other potentially toxic substances. Before they know it, many users are discovering that their e-cigarette habit has grown into a serious addiction.

Chapter Two

Why Are E-Cigarettes and Vaping So Addictive?

Health experts agree: e-cigarettes and vaping are highly addictive. Millions of addicted users have also personally discovered that it is extremely difficult to quit vaping. What makes quitting so hard? Like being addicted to cigarettes, being addicted to vaping is more than just having a physical addiction to the drug nicotine. Vaping also affects a person's behavior and emotions. If someone vapes to manage feelings and emotions, he or she may develop an emotional addiction to vaping. The vaping habit may also be linked to certain people and social activities. All of these factors play a role in addiction and explain why vaping can be extremely difficult to quit.

Nicotine's Physical Hold

Nicotine is a highly addictive drug. In fact, addiction experts rank it among the top three most addictive drugs, along with heroin and cocaine. "Nicotine is the most addictive substance known to mankind," says Richard Stumacher, the chief of the Division of Pulmonary/Critical Care at Northern Westchester Hospital. "During the nine years I spent helping people who had been addicted to crack, heroin, and alcohol stop smoking, they all said that smoking was the hardest addiction to kick."[23]

In the body, nicotine acts as both a stimulant and a sedative. As a stimulant, it speeds up one or more of the body's systems. When nicotine enters the body, a person experiences a sort of kick. The nicotine stimulates the body's adrenal glands and causes them to release the hormone epinephrine, also known as adrenaline. The adrenaline stimulates the body and triggers a release of glucose; it also increases the person's blood pressure, heart rate, and respiration. Nicotine also causes the pancreas to produce less insulin, which causes an increase in blood sugar. As more nicotine builds in the bloodstream, it can have a sedative effect on the body and slow its systems, helping a person relax and destress.

"Nicotine is the most addictive substance known to mankind."[23]

—Richard Stumacher, the chief of the Division of Pulmonary/ Critical Care at Northern Westchester Hospital

At the same time, nicotine activates the reward pathways in the brain. These pathways are connected areas of the brain that regulate feelings of pleasure and reinforce associated behaviors. Nicotine causes the brain to release dopamine, a chemical known as a neurotransmitter, to areas of the brain that control pleasure and motivation. Dopamine causes users to experience a pleasurable sensation, and these good feelings reinforce the behavior of smoking or vaping. This pleasure response of dopamine plays a significant role in becoming addicted to all drugs, including nicotine.

Nineteen-year-old college student Irvin Gaspar is familiar with the pleasure response nicotine activates in the brain. After a long day of classes, he relaxes on his couch, fills his vape pen with e-liquid, and inhales a heated strawberry-flavored vapor. When he exhales, a sweet-smelling cloud circles around his head before moving slowing toward the ceiling. Gaspar, who started vaping at age fifteen, says he vapes because it helps him relieve stress and he likes the way it feels. "Vaping takes away stress for a lot of people," says Gaspar. "It gives you a head rush, kind of like a buzz and you feel more focused."[24]

If a person does not get nicotine, however, the brain's pleasure response stops. This can cause feelings of anxiety or stress. In addition, the person may experience nicotine withdrawal symptoms,

Nicotine Triggers Reward Pathways in the Brain

Nicotine, (red triangle), causes nerve cells to release dopamine (pink dots), causing pleasurable feelings in the user. To handle the flood of dopamine, the nerve cell creates more dopamine receptors, which can lead to craving and addiction. Teen brains, which are still developing, are especially vulnerable to nicotine addiction, which can result in impaired attention, depression, and anxiety.

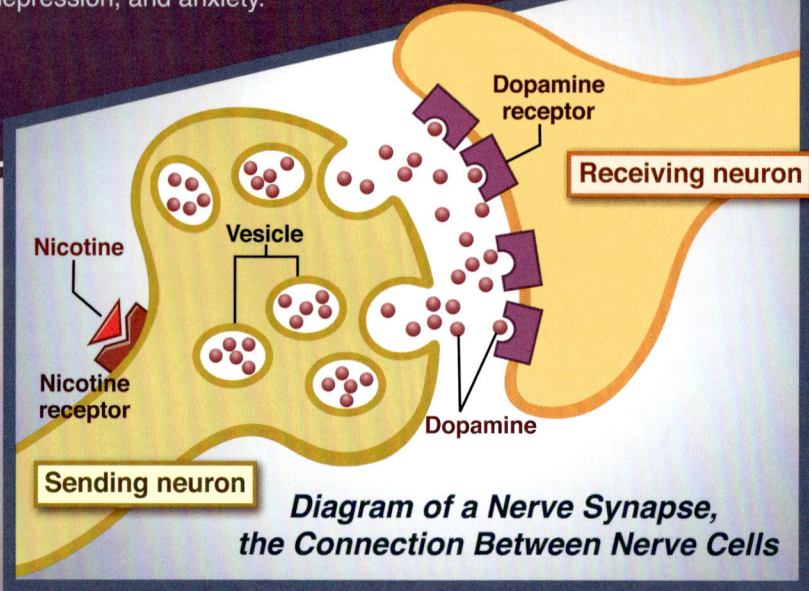

Dopamine receptor

Receiving neuron

Nicotine

Vesicle

Nicotine receptor

Dopamine

Sending neuron

Diagram of a Nerve Synapse, the Connection Between Nerve Cells

Source: Janet Raloff, "E-Cigarettes Proving to Be a Danger to Teens," *ScienceNews*, June 30, 2015. www.sciencenews.com.

which include strong cravings, irritability, restlessness, difficulty concentrating, depression, anger, and trouble sleeping. The easiest way to relieve these symptoms is to smoke or vape, which sends nicotine to the brain, releases more dopamine, and leads to pleasurable feelings. The increasing need for nicotine to generate pleasurable feelings drives the cycle of addiction.

Brain Changes: Needing More Nicotine

Every time a person vapes, nicotine enters the bloodstream and reaches the brain in seconds. Receptors in the brain absorb the nicotine, which triggers the release of feel-good dopamine. But over time, high levels of nicotine can actually cause the brain to experience changes—many of which are long lasting.

Research has shown that if a person continues to smoke over time, the number of nicotine receptors in his or her brain increases. In fact, compared to nonsmokers, addicted smokers often have billions more nicotine receptors. With more receptors present, more and more nicotine is needed to generate the same feelings of pleasure. This requires the person to smoke or vape more in order to achieve the same effect. Eventually, the body needs a constant flow of nicotine to feel good. This is how physical addiction begins. "Everybody has a certain amount of nicotine receptors in the brain," says K. Vendrell Rankin, the director of Tobacco Treatment Services at Texas A&M University's Baylor College of Dentistry. "When you start smoking, vaping, or supplying nicotine to them, they multiply."[25] The extra nicotine receptors linger for as long as six weeks after a person quits smoking, which may contribute to the powerful cravings experienced during nicotine withdrawal.

This condition is known as tolerance. The person will need to smoke or vape more in order to experience the same high from nicotine. They may have cravings or a strong desire to vape. They may find themselves reorganizing their work or social schedule around vaping. They may feel anxious or irritable if they do not vape. One of the most telling signs of addiction is that the person will continue to vape even if they know it is causing them problems and affecting their health.

Delivering Nicotine

The popular Juul e-cigarettes deliver one of the most powerful nicotine punches on the market. Each Juul pod contains fifty-nine milligrams of nicotine per milliliter of e-liquid. According to the Juul company, one pod contains the same amount of nicotine as a pack of cigarettes. However, it is difficult to compare the pod to a cigarette because not all of the nicotine in cigarette smoke is inhaled, and some remains in the cigarette's filter. Juuls also use a much more powerful nicotine delivery device, delivering nicotine in a way that is very easy for the body to absorb. This increases the risk of becoming addicted to e-cigarettes.

This was demonstrated in a 2018 study in which researchers examined how nicotine was delivered by Juul and similar e-cigarettes. They followed more than five hundred patients aged twelve to twenty-one at three Stony Brook Children's Hospital outpatient clinics in Long Island, New York. Participants answered an extensive questionnaire about their e-cigarette use, and more than half gave urine samples. The researchers measured the amount of nicotine in the e-cigarettes the patients reported using. Finally, they measured the level of nicotine in the urine samples to see how much of the nicotine was actually absorbed by the body.

A Juul's Powerful Punch

What makes a Juul e-cigarette so addictive? To start, Juul pods contain more nicotine than many other e-cigarettes on the market. Whereas each Juul contains fifty-nine milligrams of nicotine per milliliter of e-liquid, other e-cigarettes contain only about six to thirty milligrams of nicotine per milliliter. A Juul's nicotine level is three times the legal level allowed in the European Union, which is why the brand is not allowed to be sold there.

In addition, a Juul delivers its nicotine in a smooth, easy-to-absorb way. To do this, the company developed an e-liquid that contains nicotine salts. These salts are absorbed into the user's body at a higher level than nicotine from tobacco cigarettes, which gives users a head rush just like smoking tobacco. Yet unlike traditional cigarette smoke, which can cause an unpleasant feeling in the chest and lungs, nicotine salts are easier to inhale. This smoothness makes it easier for someone who has never smoked before to start vaping. A Juul's smooth yet powerful punch makes it the e-cigarette of choice for many users. It may also make it more addictive.

Juul, one of the most popular e-cigarettes, delivers one of the most powerful nicotine punches on the market. Each Juul pod contains fifty-nine milligrams of nicotine per milliliter of e-liquid.

The researchers found that nicotine concentrations in Juul and similar products ranged from twenty-three to fifty-six milligrams per milliliter. When they measured the nicotine levels in the vapor, they found it was nearly the same amount delivered by tobacco cigarettes. This is important because many e-cigarette users believe they are consuming less nicotine when vaping as compared to smoking.

Researchers also discovered that once nicotine is in the body, e-cigarette users absorbed it at a higher level than nicotine delivered by tobacco cigarettes. The researchers suspect that the form of nicotine used by Juul and other e-cigarette products is more easily absorbed by the body than tobacco forms of nicotine. "The levels of nicotine inhaled and absorbed by these pod users was alarmingly high," says study coauthor Rachel Boykan, a pediatrician at the hospital. "It's critically important that users, parents, clinicians, public health advocates and regulatory bodies be informed about how Juul and similar devices work, and how they impact the body."[26]

A Hard Habit to Break

An e-cigarette's nicotine delivery system helps explain why a vaping addiction can be so hard to break. Vaping is also very addictive because users often experience more than just a physical addiction. For many heavy users, the act of vaping is part of their daily routine. They vape at specific times of day, such as when they are relaxing after work with an alcoholic beverage, or when they first wake up in the morning. Users may also vape to cope with certain emotions, such as when they are stressed out or tired. When vaping becomes woven into a user's regular routine, it becomes a hard-to-break habit. People who regularly vape while drinking coffee may find that they pull out their Juul each morning without even thinking about it. The behavior of vaping with morning coffee is so ingrained in their daily routine that they do not even make a conscious decision to do it. Quitting, therefore, means users have to relearn the behaviors linked to vaping or change their routine, which can be exceedingly difficult.

When users regularly vape in the same situations or with the same people, they may begin to associate the pleasurable feelings generated by nicotine with those people and situations. This emotional attachment to vaping can be difficult to break. "This secondary reinforcing effect may contribute to the difficulty smokers have when trying to quit," says Nora Volkow, the director of NIDA at the National Institutes of Health. "It is not simply that they crave nicotine and feel withdrawal symptoms in its absence. It is also that other activities are not as enjoyable or motivating to them in the absence of nicotine."[27]

Making it even more difficult to quit is the fact that the brain's nicotine receptors can become conditioned to expect nicotine in certain situations. For example, if a person regularly vapes while drinking alcohol, the brain's nicotine receptors learn to anticipate the dopamine release from nicotine when alcohol enters the body. This anticipation causes an intense craving to vape, even long after the person has quit and even when she or he is doing an activity that is not related to vaping.

Social Pressures

For many users, vaping is a social activity. Some users develop friendships and social groups centered entirely around vaping. This social element is another factor that makes vaping so addictive. Even if users want to quit, temptations exist everywhere if they continue to hang out with friends who vape. "It is so addictive," says Danielle, who is addicted to her Juul. "I try to quit, but every one of my friends has one."[28]

Some teens feel intense social pressure to vape. Social groups at this age have tremendous influence over a person's choice of activities and decisions.

For teens, the social pressure to vape may be extremely intense. This is because during the teen years, friends have an enormous influence over a person's activities and interests, especially risky behavior like vaping. Teens who want to fit in with those around them will vape to project a specific image about themselves. Once addicted, teens find it even more difficult to quit because everyone around them is doing it.

A Gateway to Smoking Tobacco

Since e-cigarettes first appeared on the market, tobacco users, policy makers, and others have touted them as a smoking cessation device—that is, a way to help people quit smoking tobacco cigarettes or prevent them from starting in the first place. However, research shows that this may not be the case, especially when it comes to young people. In fact, using e-cigarettes may make it *more likely* that young adults will begin smoking tobacco cigarettes.

A December 2017 study by researchers at the University of Pittsburgh found that young adults who used e-cigarettes were more than four times as likely to begin smoking tobacco as compared to peers who did not use e-cigarettes. Study participants reported that they interchanged vaping and smoking, often because the battery on their vaping device was dead or because cigarettes were more readily available. Researchers suspect that vapers may be more likely to smoke tobacco because the behaviors are similar so vaping becomes a way into smoking harsher tobacco. "Our study finds that in nonsmokers, e-cigarettes make people more likely to start smoking," says Brian A. Primack, the director of the university's Center for Research on Media, Technology, and Health. This contradicts the conventional theory that e-cigarettes can help users quit smoking or prevent them from picking up the habit in the first place.

Quoted in University of Pittsburgh Schools of the Health Sciences, "E-Cig Use Increases Risk of Beginning Tobacco Cigarette Use in Young Adults," ScienceDaily, December 11, 2017. www.sciencedaily.com.

An Increased Addiction Risk for Teens

Teens may feel nicotine's addictive pull even more strongly than adults. This is because the adolescent brain is still developing, and using nicotine as a teen can cause brain changes that make it physically easier to become addicted to nicotine and other drugs. "I think most people realize nicotine is addictive, but I don't know if there's an understanding of just how addictive it is—particularly for youths,"[29] says Lorena M. Siqueira, the lead author of a report on nicotine, addiction, and youth released by the American Academy of Pediatrics. In addition, research shows that the earlier a person starts using nicotine, the harder it is to quit. The user is also more likely to develop a tolerance and need higher amounts of nicotine.

Vaping may even make it more likely a teen will smoke tobacco in the future. "Because nicotine has mood-elevating and addictive effects, teens who use e-cigarettes with stronger nicotine concentrations may be less willing to stop vaping and be more inclined to use other nicotine products, like conventional cigarettes," says Adam Leventhal, the director of the Health, Emotion, and Addiction Laboratory at the Keck School of Medicine of the University of Southern California (USC). In 2017, Leventhal and a team of USC researchers studied the connection between e-cigarettes and future vaping and smoking in teens. They found that teens who used e-cigarettes with higher nicotine levels were more likely to vape and also smoke tobacco cigarettes. They were also more likely to vape and smoke more frequently and in greater quantities. "We know that teens who vape e-cigarettes are much more likely to become conventional cigarette smokers,"

> "I think most people realize nicotine is addictive, but I don't know if there's an understanding of just how addictive it is—particularly for youths."[29]
>
> —Pediatrician Lorena M. Siqueira

Leventhal said. "Our study suggests that the nicotine in e-cigarettes may be a key reason why teens who vape progress to more frequent smoking."[30]

Not everyone who uses e-cigarettes becomes addicted; however, those who do often discover that breaking the habit is extremely difficult. Nicotine is one of the world's most addictive drugs, exerting a physical hold on users that causes them to crave more of the drug. Vaping become an even harder habit to break because it becomes a routine behavior, integrated into a person's daily life. As a result, many who start vaping discover that they cannot stop.

Chapter Three

How People Become Addicted to E-Cigarettes and Vaping

Although not everyone who uses e-cigarettes becomes addicted to them, those users who do have a hard time stopping their use. How each person starts down the path of e-cigarette addiction, and why they decide to vape, differs according to the individual. Some users try e-cigarettes to experiment with friends or fit in socially. Some are enticed by the product's many flavors and flashy, hip marketing campaigns. Others turn to vaping as an alternative to traditional smoking. Regardless of how or why they originally took up e-cigarettes, regular use often leads to the same state of addiction.

Experimenting with Friends

A person's teenage years are typically a time of trying out new things, from different hairstyles and clothing to experimenting with alcohol and drugs. The same is true of e-cigarettes. Teens see their friends or perhaps the adults in their lives smoking e-cigarettes, and they want to try them too. Once a teen experiments with vaping, he or she can quickly become a regular user.

"What we are seeing is a generation of young people not just trying a product but becoming addicted to a product,"[31] says Matthew Myers, the head of the Campaign for Tobacco-Free Kids.

In the summer of 2016, seventeen-year-old Matt Murphy first experimented with e-cigarettes at a high school party. In

A person's teenage years are typically a time of trying out new things. They see their friends or perhaps adults in their lives smoking e-cigarettes and decide they want to try it.

a basement filled with teens, alcohol, and loud music, a friend offered him a hit on his Juul. At first, Murphy was skeptical. It looked like a computer flash drive, and he was not sure about inhaling whatever was in it. His friend urged him to try it and assured Murphy that it was awesome. So, Murphy put the device to his lips and drew a minty cloud into his mouth. He held the moist vapor in his mouth, pushed it to the back of his throat, and let it fill his lungs. He felt the powerful punch of the nicotine immediately, something he describes as a head rush. "It was love at first puff,"[32] says Murphy.

The next day, Murphy asked his friend if he could take a hit on the Juul again. Then he asked again the day after and the day after that. Soon, he was trying to get a hit on a Juul several times a day, because he loved the feeling it gave him. In this way, Murphy started down the path toward a serious nicotine addiction. After a few weeks of borrowing his friends' Juuls, Murphy went on a family vacation. After two days without a Juul, he craved a hit. By the third day, he was desperate. He took an Uber to a local store that sold Juuls, spending $100 on the ride and his new Juul starter kit.

Soon, Murphy was using one Juul pod a day, sometimes more. His habit cost him forty dollars per week, sucking up his savings and his paycheck from a part-time job at a local restaurant. Throughout his high school years, Murphy had successfully stayed away from marijuana, alcohol, and cigarettes. Now he was becoming dependent on vaping and nicotine. It became part of his identity and a way to bond with his friends. Together, they would ride around town while vaping in a friend's car. By the time Murphy graduated from high school in 2017, four of his five best friends also used Juuls on a daily basis.

While in college, Murphy began to realize that he had a problem. When he felt overwhelmed by his coursework at the University of Vermont, his Juul was the only way he could escape the stress. He tried to limit how much he used it by keeping it in his dorm room instead of carrying it around campus. However, it just made him want to be in his room all the time. By this point, Murphy needed to vape to manage his cravings or he would become irritable. He even attached a Velcro strip to the dresser next to his bed and attached his Juul to it, so he could grab a quick hit the moment he woke up each day. He knew that he had a problem, but did not know what to do about it. "Matt was open about wishing he didn't do it," says Tucker Houston, Murphy's freshman roommate. "It was a constant battle for him. People would tell him that they'd want to buy a Juul and he'd be like, 'No! You don't want to, it's not cool, it's not fun.' He became known as the juuling anti-Juul advocate."[33]

When Murphy went home for the summer, his mother discovered his Juul and empty pods in his bedroom. Murphy's parents were shocked by how much their son was vaping and the effort he had put into hiding the habit from them. They confronted Murphy and told him that he had to stop vaping. Although the confrontation with his parents was difficult, it led Murphy to realize that he indeed needed to quit. "I could not justify the addiction anymore. And I realized my parents were my allies. Because I wanted to stop and they wanted me to stop,"[34] he says.

Breaking a powerful nicotine addiction was not easy. Murphy tried to wean off his Juul, taking longer breaks between hits. He experienced withdrawal symptoms, including anxiety and the shakes. It was also difficult to be with his friends because they continued to vape. "When Matt withdrew, he'd flip out a lot, especially when other people had it around him," says Jared Stack, a friend. "They wouldn't stop doing it just because he had. They didn't care—because they were addicted too."[35]

After three weeks, the worst of Murphy's withdrawal symptoms passed. He transferred to a school closer to home and had not vaped for almost six months. He still feels the urge to vape, but he reminds himself about how difficult it was to live with his nicotine addiction. Like thousands of teens, Murphy's decision to experiment and vape with friends led to addiction.

A Harmless Habit?

Many others start using e-cigarettes because they view it as something new and exciting. They see it as a novelty product, something cleaner and more fun than traditional cigarettes. In fact, according to the 2016 National Youth Tobacco Survey, 17 percent of high school and middle school students who tried e-cigarettes said they did so because they believed they were less harmful than tobacco. "A lot of our kids do not see the harm," says Nancy Voise, an assistant superintendent with the Naperville Community Unit School District 203 in Illinois. "It's trendy as a fad."[36]

The Legal Vaping Age

In most states, the legal age to purchase e-cigarettes is eighteen (the same as traditional cigarettes). Some states, including California, Hawaii, Oregon, New Jersey, and Maine, have raised the legal age to purchase e-cigarettes to twenty-one. A few states—Alabama, Alaska, and Utah—use a legal age of nineteen.

Despite these age restrictions, teens are still getting their hands on e-cigarettes. In April 2018 the Truth Initiative conducted a national survey of more than one thousand twelve- to seventeen-year-olds who admitted to using e-cigarettes in the past thirty days to find out where they were getting their supply. In the survey, teens could select more than one answer. The majority, 74 percent, said they got their e-cigarettes from a physical store, such as a convenience store or a gas station. Although these outlets are not supposed to sell to minors, many did not verify their customers' ages. More than half of the teens, 52 percent, reported they got e-cigarettes from someone they knew, such as a family member or friend. Only 6 percent reported that they used the Internet to order e-cigarettes, but those who did were rarely asked to prove their age.

In 2018 the FDA sent warning letters to physical and online retailers of e-cigarettes for selling these products to minors. If the retailers do not stop selling to minors, they may face steep financial penalties and other punitive action.

Caleb Beck is one such teen. He started using e-cigarettes when he was seventeen. At first, he and his friends would pass around an e-cigarette they took from one of their fathers. Then they went online to search new vapes and flavors, such as green apple and graham cracker. For them, vaping was a novelty. Beck and his friends thought it was a way to get a nicotine buzz without the cancer risk that came with smoking tobacco cigarettes. "Cigarettes seemed like a really terrible, stigmatized thing, something you should never do," says Beck. "But having . . . something cleaner, with more flavors—well that was enough for me and my friends to buy e-cigarettes."[37]

Before long, Beck's casual vaping had turned into regular use. He started craving vapes and got anxious when he could not get his nicotine fix. "I'd wake up just feeling brittle," he says. "And my mood would shift if I was separated from it. You just get fixated on it."[38] By the time he was eighteen, Beck was buying disposable e-cigarettes, going through his supply every few days. When he started college, his nicotine dependence led him to start smoking traditional cigarettes, which were cheaper than e-cigarettes. However, his nicotine addiction became even stronger. Beck thought that maybe he could go back to vaping in an attempt to quit traditional cigarettes. This time, he bought a Juul to deliver his nicotine

Teens often see regular cigarettes as gross and harmful. E-cigarettes seem cleaner and more appealing to them with all the fun flavors.

rush. Although he hoped to quit nicotine entirely, his Juul delivered even more nicotine than the e-cigarettes he had originally used. Beck's harmless habit had turned into a full-fledged addiction.

Erin Brock also believed vaping was harmless. While in college, she occasionally smoked when having a drink at a party. Tobacco products did not appeal to her; she worried about the health risks of cigarettes, and she did not like the smell of tobacco or its aftertaste. When she tried a Juul, however, she liked it immediately. The vaping device gave her a big head rush without any of the smell associated with smoking. Juul e-liquids also came in appealing flavors like mint and fruit medley. "Everyone at the bar had Juuls, literally everyone," she says. "Everyone had different flavors."[39] She got caught up in what she calls the vaping culture. This involved sharing Juuls with friends at parties, posting photos on social media, and making jokes about being addicted to the pocket-sized device.

Within a few months of regular use, however, Brock had developed a full-blown nicotine addiction. "I moved from taking it to go out to hitting it in my room, to taking it to school, to taking it to work, I ended up just literally always having it on me," she says. "It made me feel bad, it made me feel gross. I was embarrassed because it wasn't a joke anymore. . . . I never wanted to have a nicotine addiction." For Brock, the cost of her nicotine addiction became overwhelming. A Juul device costs about thirty-five dollars, and a pack of four pods sells for about sixteen dollars. At her peak, Brock was using a pod a day. "I actually ended up quitting just because I was, like, I can't afford this anymore," she says, "and . . . I was getting pretty grossed out at how much I felt I needed it." While breaking her addiction was a challenge, Brock is happier without her Juul. "Quitting [is hard], but I'm glad I'm not addicted to a USB stick,"[40] she says.

A Way to Stop Smoking

An estimated 34.3 million adults in the United States smoked cigarettes in 2017, according to the CDC. Nearly seven out of ten smokers say they want to quit, according to Johns Hopkins Medicine. Some smokers try to quit cold turkey, but others turn to smoking cessation aids such as nicotine patches or gum. With the rise in popularity of e-cigarettes, some smokers think vaping might be a way to kick their tobacco habit. Although e-cigarettes are not approved by the FDA as a smoking cessation aid, some vaping companies, such as Juul, have promoted their products as a less risky alternative to smoking. For example, the Juul website urges smokers to "Make the Switch." It also says that "Juul was developed as a satisfying alternative to cigarettes. Learn about our mission to improve the lives of the world's one billion adult smokers by eliminating cigarettes."[41]

> "It was supposed to be a transitional thing to get off what vapers refer to as the analogs—cigarettes—but it's been over two years, and we're still vaping."[42]
>
> —Christian Mazza, e-cigarette user

Video director Christian Mazza is one person who was initially swayed by this message. He had smoked cigarettes for fifteen years when he decided to try e-cigarettes to replace smoking. He did not like the Juul at first, but over time "it just sort of took over," he says. Yet Mazza admits that once he and his wife made the switch from smoking tobacco to e-cigarettes, they found it hard to stop vaping. "It was supposed to be a transitional thing to get off what vapers refer to as the analogs—cigarettes—but it's been over two years, and we're still vaping," says Mazza about the couple's attempt to quit smoking. "At what point does the transition get us off of nicotine completely?"[42]

Martha de Lacey also tried e-cigarettes as a way to cut down on the social smoking she did when out with friends. She was curious about the feel, taste, and smell of e-cigarettes. At the time, she believed there was little harm in trying them. "If someone had warned me quite how addictive e-cigarettes would be, I'd never have taken my first puff. I had no idea how sweet a

Risk Factors for Addiction

Anyone who uses e-cigarettes or nicotine products can develop a nicotine addiction. However, not everyone who vapes becomes addicted. Certain factors will increase a person's risk of addiction.

Genetics plays a role in who becomes addicted to nicotine. Multiple genes may influence how brain receptors react to high doses of nicotine, and they can make someone more (or less) likely to develop an addiction. A person's family history also matters. Someone who grows up in a home with tobacco users is more likely to use tobacco and e-cigarettes than someone who grows up in a tobacco-free home. Age is another risk factor. The younger people are when they start vaping, the more likely they are to develop an addiction. Finally, people who already have a substance abuse problem (with alcohol or drugs) or who are struggling with mental illness are also more likely to become dependent on nicotine.

mouthful of warm, flavored vapor followed by a little nicotine rush could be. Especially when it comes without that familiar stench of ashtray,"[43] she says.

A Complicated Role in Quitting Tobacco

Do e-cigarettes actually help smokers quit? It depends. Most researchers and health professionals agree that for adults, e-cigarettes are ultimately less harmful because they do not contain tobacco, which is responsible for many of the negative health effects of smoking. Therefore, when used as a complete replacement for smoking, e-cigarettes can be an improvement for smokers who have been unable to quit using other methods but do not plan to stop using nicotine.

However, for smokers who want to cut down on or quit nicotine entirely, the use

"If someone had warned me quite how addictive e-cigarettes would be, I'd never have taken my first puff."[43]

—Martha de Lacey, e-cigarette user

of e-cigarettes and vaping may not be as effective. This is because e-cigarettes simply support a person's nicotine addiction or transfer it to a different delivery system. "One of the major reasons people use e-cigarettes, especially adults, is because they think they'll help them try to quit," says Stanton Glantz, the director of the Center for Tobacco Control Research and Education at the University of California, San Francisco (UCSF). "For most people they actually make it harder to quit."[44]

Indeed, some studies have shown that e-cigarettes do not help users stop smoking. In a 2018 study, researchers at UCSF

found that cigarette smokers did *not* smoke fewer cigarettes when they started using e-cigarettes. Instead, many smokers simply became users of both types of cigarettes (known as dual users). In the study, dual users and cigarette-only smokers reported how many cigarettes they smoked. The median number of cigarettes—the middle number in the list of responses—was one more cigarette per day for dual users as compared to cigarette-only users. In addition, compared to the smokers, dual users reported lower general health, increased breathing problems, higher depression and anxiety, and lower physical activity. "While some may view e-cigarettes as a means to quit or reduce smoking, instead these devices may simply add yet more toxic exposure on top of conventional cigarettes,"[45] says senior author Gregory Marcus, a cardiologist and the director of clinical research for UCSF's Division of Cardiology.

> "One of the major reasons people use e-cigarettes, especially adults, is because they think they'll help them try to quit. For most people they actually make it harder to quit."[44]
>
> —Stanton Glantz, the director of the Center for Tobacco Control Research and Education at UCSF

Regular Use Leads to Addiction

No matter how someone starts using e-cigarettes and other vaping devices, the path to addiction is similar: occasional use quickly turns to regular use, and vapers soon finds themselves craving their next hit or becoming irritable when they cannot vape. "If you try e-cigarettes for whatever reason, the risk is that it has nicotine and it's very addictive," says Curtis Turner, a professor of pediatrics at the University of South Alabama College of Medicine. "[You] get addicted for life."[46]

Chapter Four

Affecting Lives

For those who become addicted to e-cigarettes and vaping, what starts out as a harmless habit can end up deteriorating many aspects of their lives. From their physical and mental health to their relationships with others, e-cigarettes and vaping can have a lasting impact. Often, users do not realize the impact of e-cigarettes on their lives until they are addicted. "The main problem of vape products is we don't see the same level of perception of harm with either parents or kids," says Matt Cassity, a project coordinator for a youth services organization in Naperville, Illinois. "The vast majority of them have no idea about e-juice. It's water vapor rather than smoke. It doesn't mean there's no harm. The majority of students make their decision [to vape] based on the false belief it's harmless."[47]

Colorado State University student Julien Lavandier started using e-cigarettes in tenth grade. Now he is addicted and has not been able to quit. "Believe it," says the now twenty-one-year-old Lavandier. "It's a habit for me, you know—all the time when I set down my schoolwork to do homework, take a rip of the Juul. When I get in my car, take a rip of the Juul."[48] Lavandier started vaping at high school parties where everyone was doing it. E-cigarettes looked cool and fun, and they seemed harmless.

Before long, Lavandier moved from vaping occasionally at parties to smoking e-cigarettes regularly. To get his nicotine fix, he started smoking tobacco cigarettes, even though he had not been a smoker before he started vaping. He tried a Juul and found it even more habit forming than a regular e-cigarette. "It's impossible to let go once you started using," Lavandier says. "I'll

tell you—after even an hour and a half or two, I am chomping at the bit to find my Juul."[49] On a typical day, Lavandier estimates that he takes about three hundred puffs on his Juul. He unsuccessfully tried to quit but failed to go three days without vaping.

Oral Health Risks

Because vaping is relatively new, scientists are just beginning to research its effects on the human body. While the results of long-term studies are not yet available, there is increasing concern over the health risks that have been linked to e-cigarettes and vaping. One is the risk to oral health. Some users report experiencing inflammation in their mouth and throat, mouth sores, and other oral problems after repeatedly vaping.

When Irfan Rahman, a toxicologist at the University of Rochester, spoke to young people who vaped regularly, he discovered that many of them complained of bleeding mouths and throats. The bloody mouth sores were particularly slow to heal. Concerned, Rahman decided to study what effect the vapors from e-cigarettes had on mouth cells. In the study, Rahman and his team exposed gum tissue from nonsmokers to e-cigarette vapor. They found that the vapors caused inflammation and damaged the cells. "We showed that when the vapors from an e-cigarette are burned, it causes cells to release inflammatory proteins, which in turn aggravate stress within cells, resulting in damage that could lead to various oral diseases," says Rahman. "How much and how often someone is smoking e-cigarettes will determine the extent of damage to the gums and oral cavity."[50]

The study also found that chemicals in e-cigarette flavorings play a role in damaging mouth cells. "We learned that the

"We showed that when the vapors from an e-cigarette are burned, it causes cells to release inflammatory proteins, which in turn aggravate stress within cells, resulting in damage that could lead to various oral diseases."[50]

—Irfan Rahman, a toxicologist at the University of Rochester

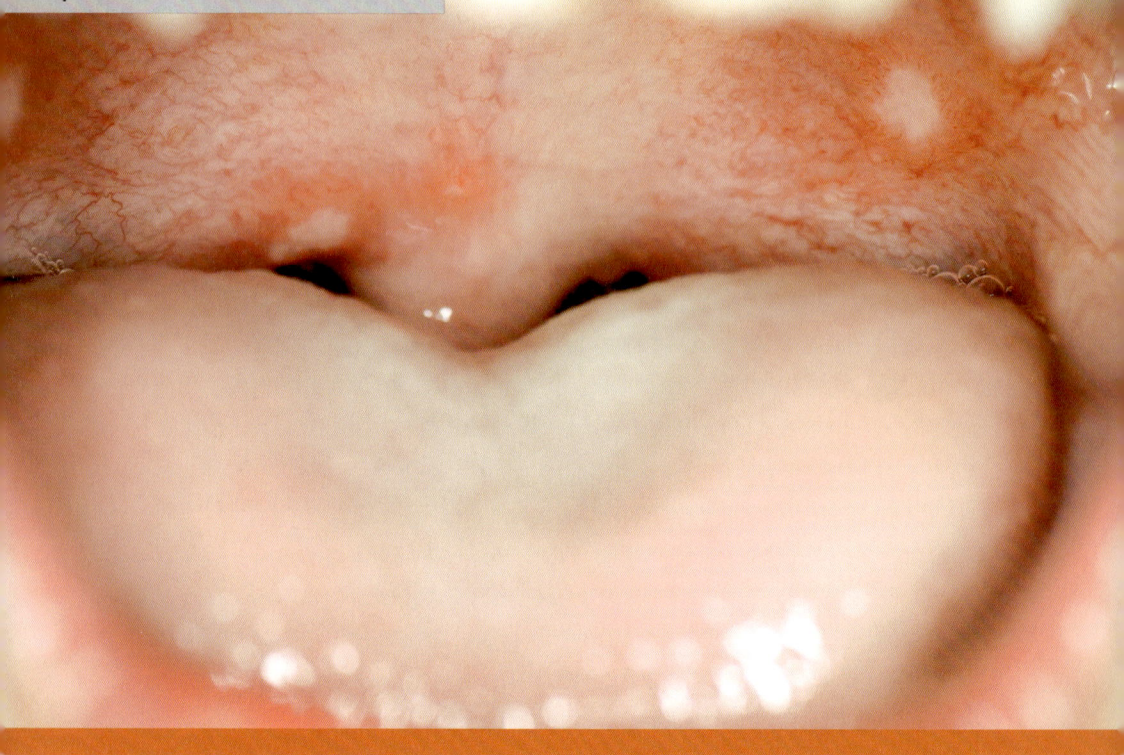

There is concern over the impact e-cigarettes can have on oral health. Some users report inflammation of the mouth and throat, mouth sores, and other oral problems like those shown here.

flavorings—some more than others—made the damage to the cells even worse," says Fawad Javed, a postdoctoral student at the Eastman Institute for Oral Health, who contributed to the study. "It's important to remember that e-cigarettes contain nicotine, which is known to contribute to gum disease."[51] Over time, inflammation in the cells lining the mouth can lead to bleeding mouth sores and sore throats. The inflammation can also lead to gum disease, which destroys the gum tissue that hold teeth in place. If gum disease becomes severe enough, it can lead to tooth loss.

Lung Health

The vapors that damage the lining of the mouth and throat can also inflame and damage lung tissue. A 2018 study published online in the journal *Thorax* found that e-cigarette vapor increases the production of inflammatory chemicals and disables important protective cells in the lungs that keep them clear of harmful particles. The findings suggest that some of the effects of e-cigarettes are similar to those lung effects seen in regular smokers and people with chronic lung disease.

When users inhale vapor particles, they irritate the lungs. The lungs respond by creating mucus to trap the irritating particles, which triggers a recurring cough in an attempt to clear the mucus. Over time, repeatedly inhaling the particles can lead to a lung inflamation called bronchitis, which causes chronic wheezing and a persistent cough. Although the flu and other infections can cause bronchitis, so, too, can inhaling pollution, tobacco smoke, and other chemical fumes. Bronchitis symptoms that do not go away become chronic bronchitis. Cigarette smoking is the most common cause of chronic bronchitis—and now vaping may also be a cause.

To study vaping and lung health, researchers at USC spoke to about two thousand high school students about their vaping habits. They asked the teens about any respiratory symptoms they had experienced, including coughing or phlegm. Students who reported a daily cough for at least three straight months were considered to have chronic bronchitis. Students with persistent phlegm or congestion for three or more months without a cold or flu were also suspected of having chronic bronchitis. Students who had vaped within the past thirty days were twice as likely to have chronic bronchitis as students who had never vaped. Even students who had vaped previously but not in the past thirty days were more likely to have chronic bronchitis than students who had never vaped. It is known that cigarette smokers with chronic bronchitis often develop permanent lung damage. Although it is too soon to know whether vaping will lead to permanent lung damage, preliminary studies suggest that this could well be the case.

In one extreme case, an eighteen-year-old Pennsylvania woman developed a severe lung condition after only three weeks of vaping. She went to the emergency room with a troubling cough, difficulty breathing, and stabbing chest pains. Doctors admitted her to the intensive care unit and put her on antibiotics. Her condition quickly worsened, and she experienced respiratory failure. Doctors put her on a breathing machine and inserted tubes into her chest to drain fluid from her lungs. They diagnosed her with hypersensitivity pneumonitis, or "wet lung," a rare immune system disorder. Wet lung causes a person's lungs to become inflamed due to an allergic reaction to inhaled dust or chemicals.

Casey Sommerfeld, the woman's doctor, said chemicals in the e-cigarettes led to the lung damage, which triggered the woman's body to mount an immune response. After being treated with drugs, she improved and was removed from the breathing machine. "It is difficult to speculate on how frequently this could happen," Sommerfeld says. "As electronic cigarette use increases, we will be seeing more case reports and side effects."[52]

Facing Consequences

A number of people start using e-cigarettes and vaping because it is a social activity. At parties and gatherings, everyone seems to be doing it, and they succumb to peer pressure. But once addiction takes hold, an e-cigarette habit is no party. Users find themselves craving a hit more and more frequently. The cravings become so strong that users cannot make it through an entire day at school or work. When caught using in places where vaping is banned, they face the consequences.

As the risks of e-cigarettes and vaping have become well known, more schools across the country have banned their use on campus. Addicted students who sneak into bathrooms or hallways to smoke an e-cigarette risk being caught by teachers or school officials. If caught, they face varying punishments including suspension.

At Cape Elizabeth High School in Maine, one student who had been caught vaping sat in the vice principal's office waiting to hear his punishment. He had already been caught vaping in school three previous times. Ashamed, the student admitted that he was addicted to vaping. "I can't stop,"[53] he told the vice principal.

Dripping Increases Health Risks

A dangerous new vaping trend called dripping may make e-cigarettes even more harmful to one's health. In the normal vaping process, e-cigarettes slowly release e-liquid from a wick onto a hot coil within the device. Dripping, however, is the practice of dropping e-liquid directly onto the device's hot coils. Dripping produces a thicker, more flavorful vapor and gives a stronger sensation in the throat. It heats the e-liquid to higher temperatures than regular e-cigarette use. Higher temperatures, however, are harmful because they produce greater emissions and expose users to harmful chemicals such as formaldehyde and acetaldehyde, which are known to cause cancer. They also expose users to higher levels of nicotine, making dripping a potentially more addictive delivery system. Despite these risks, one in four teens who vape say they have tried dripping, according to a 2017 study published in the journal *Pediatrics*.

Along with being suspended from classes, some students caught vaping at school can also be suspended from participating in athletics or other extracurricular activities. In North Jersey's Ramsey School District, students caught with vaping devices on school property are suspended for five days for the first offense and not allowed to participate in any extracurricular activities for seven days, including events like graduation and prom. At Hoover High in Canton, Ohio, football player A.J. Vega was caught at school with an e-cigarette in 2017, which violated school policy. "A.J. was playing basketball at the school and a vape pen . . . fell out of his pocket," says family attorney Warner Mendenhall. "One of the coaches came up. They asked him, 'Is this yours?' He admitted it."[54] The football team suspended Vega for the remainder of the season.

People who cannot control their urge to vape can even find themselves in trouble with the law. For example, the use of e-cigarettes or other vaping devices is banned on airplanes. However, that does not stop addicted users from trying to sneak a puff or two, especially if the flight is long. If caught, vaping passengers

Using e-cigarettes or other vaping devices is banned on airplanes. That does not stop some addicted users from trying to sneak a puff or two, especially if the flight is long.

risk getting kicked off the flight. In 2018 a man allegedly smoked an e-cigarette as he waited in line on the ramp to board his flight. After being confronted by the plane's flight attendant and pilot, the man was not allowed to board.

Meanwhile, in 2015, thirty-four-year-old realtor Kristin Sharp faced possible federal charges after an altercation with a flight attendant over her vaping on a flight from Las Vegas to Honolulu. Witnesses say the flight attendant asked Sharp to put away her vape pen as she entered the plane, which she did. Later in the flight, she took out the vape pen and used it in her seat and in the bathroom. When a flight attendant asked Sharp to stop vaping, other passengers on the flight say Sharp became belligerent. Now she faces potential federal charges for interfering with a flight attendant.

Consuming Lives

Living with an addiction to e-cigarettes can become all-consuming. Users plan their day around when they can get their next fix of nicotine. In 2017 Ahmed Kabil decided to try a Juul as a way to wean himself off his cigarette habit. "Soon enough, I found I preferred the experience of Juuling to tobacco. Within three weeks, I quit smoking cigarettes without even meaning to,"[55] says Kabil. Friends congratulated him on being able to quit smoking and making a healthier choice. Kabil's wife, however, warned him that vaping carried its own risks.

Kabil later realized that he was getting more and more consumed by his vaping habit. Cigarettes, he says, have built-in limits because of the inconvenience of finding a place to smoke and the way tobacco is packed into single-serving cigarettes. Vape devices do not have these limits, which makes it easier for them to take over a person's life. "Over time, I realized I was Juuling far more than I ever smoked," says Kabil. "I Juuled at my desk, in the bathroom, on the phone, at the dinner table, and while laying in bed. I was flooding my system with nicotine and could scarcely go more than a few minutes before the desire to Juul rose from my [subconscious] and punctuated every third thought. It was the last thing I thought about before I went to bed and the first thing I thought about when I woke up."[56]

After moving to Barcelona, Spain, Kabil panicked when he noticed that his supply of Juul pods was getting low. In Spain, Juul devices are banned because of their high nicotine content. Now his days center on making his supply last as long as possible and coming up with a plan to get more pods. "Because Juul doesn't intoxicate me, I appear fine on the surface," he says. "But internally, I am suf-

> "I am a Juul junkie, a ghost with a hunger I can't ever satisfy."[57]
>
> —Ahmed Kabil, e-cigarette addict

fering through the moment-to-moment unfolding of my days, fixating on that next drag. And as the supplies dwindle to zero, the looming threat of Juul's deprivation, and its eventual absence, turns me into somebody I don't recognize. I am a Juul junkie, a ghost with a hunger I can't ever satisfy."[57]

A Rise in Nicotine Poisoning

Until recent years, nicotine poisoning was rare and not necessarily related to smoking; it was usually linked to being exposed to insecticides, whose active ingredient is high levels of nicotine. With the introduction of e-cigarettes and Juul pods, however, nicotine poisoning cases have increased. In 2011 poison control centers received just 269 calls related to nicotine poisoning, according to the American Association of Poison Control Centers. Just seven years later, in 2018, poison control centers received 3,137 calls involving nicotine poisoning.

Nicotine poisoning is caused by overexposure to nicotine. This can occur by inhaling or ingesting nicotine, or absorbing it through the skin or eyes. The e-liquids in e-cigarettes are the cause of the majority of nicotine poisoning cases.

Symptoms of nicotine poisoning generally occur in two stages. Within the first hour of poisoning, a person may experience nausea, stomachache, watering of the mouth, heavy breathing, faster heartbeat, increased blood pressure, pale skin, headache, and dizziness. In the second stage, which occurs thirty minutes to four hours after poisoning, the person may experience shallow breathing, slower heartbeat, diarrhea, lethargy, weakness, and seizures. If someone with these symptoms suspects nicotine poisoning, he or she should call poison control immediately.

Changing Behavior

Some e-cigarette addicts become nearly unrecognizable to their family and friends. In high school, Luka Kinard first started vaping because he saw older students doing it and thought it would make him fit in. He picked a Juul because he thought it was healthier than smoking cigarettes and did not have their telltale smell. As he began to vape regularly, Kinard's behavior started to change. His grades dropped, and he stopped participating in activities that he had enjoyed, such as Boy Scouts and fishing. Instead, he spent all his time locked in his room vaping. "He went from being a straight-A student to an F student," says his mother, Kelly Kinard. "(It was) a very rapid decline in grades. His behavior became explosive. He was very angry and it just wasn't him."[58]

Kinard's vaping habit soon became expensive, costing him $150 a week for pods. "I was selling my clothes," says the fifteen-year-old. "I would get shoes, sell them, go out get cheap shoes, sell them. I was doing anything and everything to get money."[59] When he had a seizure at his girlfriend's house after vaping, Kinard could no longer hide his addiction from his parents. After some research, Kinard's parents sent him to a forty-day addiction rehabilitation program. The program helped him kick his vaping habit and return to his normal life.

Damaging Relationships

Like many other addictions, an e-cigarette and vaping dependency can damage a person's relationships with family and friends. When craving their next puff on an e-cigarette, users can become irritable and snap at those around them. Those who hide their habit may withdraw from others and spend more time alone. They may even steal from loved ones in order to finance their habit.

An addiction to e-cigarettes and vaping can damage a person's relationships with family and friends. When craving their next puff, users can become irritable and snap at those around them.

When interviewed in 2017, a fifteen-year-old Juul addict from Kalamazoo, Michigan, admitted that he could not go an hour without hitting his Juul. When unable to do so, he says, "I get really short with people. The only thing on my mind is *how can I get pods? How can I tell my parents I'm going somewhere else? When can I get them?*" When he is with his parents, he goes to the bathroom to get a hit. "If I'm in a situation where I'm with a bunch of people and there's no way I can turn my back or anything, I go to the bathroom," he says. The teen admits that he has done some things that he regrets to get pods. "I stole money from my parents once. Out of their wallet. I'm not super mean to people or anything. I've been one day without pods since the beginning of the year. For the last three months I've been one a day, so it's like a pack of cigarettes every day. I kind of stop everything else everyone is doing and try and get pods, that's something I regret,"[60] he says.

Addiction's Impact

Being addicted to e-cigarettes can upend people's lives. They may suffer health problems, such as bleeding mouth sores and lung damage. As addiction's grip tightens, they may find themselves consumed with getting their next hit at the expense of their loved ones. And if the need to vape drives them to break workplace or school rules, they may find themselves facing the consequences.

Chapter Five

Overcoming E-Cigarette and Vaping Addiction

Overcoming an addiction to e-cigarettes and vaping is a significant challenge for anyone. Users must endure physical withdrawal symptoms such as headaches and cravings. Because vaping has become so embedded in their daily lives, users may have to change their day-to-day routines to avoid people, places, and situations that trigger their desire to vape. Andrea "Nick" Tattanelli, who quit vaping in 2018, succinctly sums up the experience in the following way: "It was hell."[61]

The Pain of Withdrawal

Nicotine causes severe physical and psychological addiction. When users stop vaping, they experience physical withdrawal symptoms as nicotine leaves their body. These symptoms usually include headaches, sweating, restlessness, tremors, insomnia, increased appetite, nausea, and digestive problems. Although uncomfortable, these physical effects are not life threatening. They tend to peak over one to three days after quitting and then decrease over a period of three to four weeks. At that point, the person has eliminated nicotine from his or her body. However, the psychological withdrawal effects can last much longer than the physical ones. These include very powerful nicotine cravings, irritability, depression, mood swings, and difficulty concentrating. Every person has a different experience withdrawing from nicotine. Some people experience physical side effects very intensely and for several weeks; others experience symptoms for just a few days but struggle with the more psychological elements of addiction.

At the peak of his e-cigarette addiction, twenty-five-year-old Elvijs Arnicans used to vape every ten to twenty minutes. Sometimes, he even fell asleep with his vaping device in his hand. When he decided to quit, he was surprised at how difficult it was. For the first three days of withdrawal, Arnicans felt extremely tired and

When users stop vaping, they will experience nicotine withdrawal symptoms. These symptoms can include headaches, nausea, sweating, and insomnia.

found it difficult to concentrate. "It was awful. I feel like my brain gets turned down and only works at about 20 percent capability," he says. As his brain fog cleared, cravings to vape intensified and Arnicans struggled to enjoy his daily activities. "I found myself unconsciously reaching for my vape [device] every 10 minutes or so," he says. "I found it incredibly difficult to concentrate on simple tasks."[62]

University of Massachusetts student Maxwell Zeff encountered similar problems when he decided to quit vaping in 2018. "I was tired of being controlled by something so destructive and I decided to not buy another pack of Juul pods once I ran out," he says. The next week, Zeff struggled with withdrawal symptoms. At one point, his nicotine cravings were so intense that he skipped class because he was unable to focus on anything but his need for nicotine. "I never imagined I would be experiencing nicotine withdrawal at any point in my life, but especially not at the young age of 18." After the first week of quitting, Zeff's physical symptoms subsided but his mental cravings continued. Given his experience, he regards quitting vaping as even more difficult than quitting tobacco because of the way in which vaping is embraced by young people. "If I had been addicted to smoking cigarettes, I would've been ostracized by even my closest peers," he says. "Every time I would've taken out a cigarette, I would have been met with vocal and implicit ridicule by everyone around me. But Juuling has become an accepted practice that is almost impossible to escape in college. It happens at the parties, on the sidewalks, in dorm rooms and everywhere you can think of."[63] Vaping's widespread practice among youth—and their ignorance about its addictive potential and health risks—are among the things that public health experts and others are trying to change.

> "I never imagined I would be experiencing nicotine withdrawal at any point in my life, but especially not at the young age of 18."[63]
>
> —Maxwell Zeff, e-cigarette user

Few Approved Treatments Are Available

Because vaping is so new and still evolving, there is little scientific evidence to establish which treatments best help people quit. When a person wants to quit smoking tobacco cigarettes, health professionals can recommend clear treatments and methods. Some smokers quit cold turkey, but others wean themselves slowly off cigarettes by systematically reducing the number they smoke each day. Others use nicotine replacement therapy (NRT) to help them get through the first few days of withdrawal. NRTs include skin patches, nicotine gum, lozenges, nasal sprays, and inhalers. NRTs supply smokers with a controlled dose of nicotine as they slowly wean off the drug. For those who experience more severe withdrawal symptoms, some medications can effectively reduce cravings and block the brain's reward system for smoking.

Vape Detectors Sound the Alarm

Some high schools are using vape detectors—devices similar to smoke detectors—to curb vaping in school bathrooms. Fly Sense detection devices are hardwired sensors that detect chemicals emitted during vaping. When the device senses the chemicals, it sends a real-time alert to school officials. The officials can hurry to the bathroom to catch students as they vape. If security video is available, officials can review it to identify who entered and exited the bathroom at the time the sensor alerted.

According to Derek Peterson, the founder and chief executive officer of Soter Technologies, the company that makes Fly Sense, hundreds of school districts in twenty-one states and Canada have bought the vaping detection device. In Massachusetts, Georgetown High School and Middle School installed ten sensors in bathrooms in September 2018. The school's assistant principal, Maria Lysen, believes the detection devices are working as an effective vaping deterrent. Since they were installed on the bathroom ceilings, reports of vaping have declined in her school. The school plans to install another ten detectors in the future.

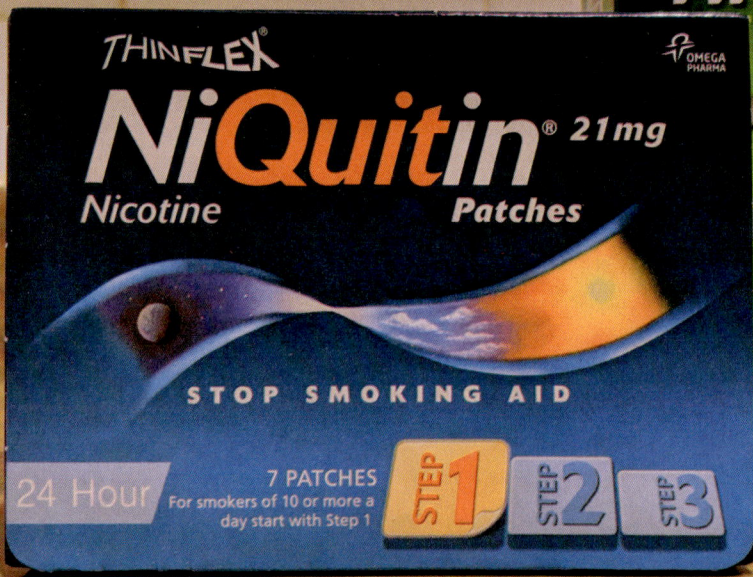

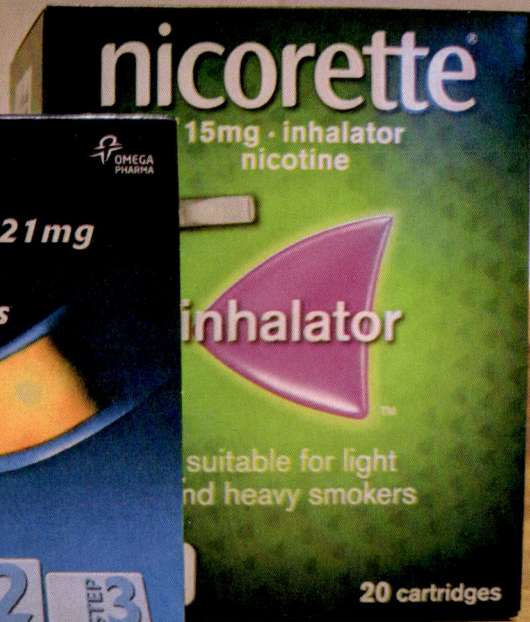

Smokers trying to quit may use nicotine replacement therapies such as nicotine patches and inhalers. These aids supply a person with a controlled dose of nicotine as they slowly wean off the drug.

However, public health experts are struggling to help vapers quit their habit. Traditional tobacco cessation methods do not translate well to vaping because it is difficult to measure the amount of nicotine each person inhales and absorbs through e-cigarettes. In addition, NRTs and smoking cessation medications are only available for adults and are not approved for use by teens. Even when used, these patches and prescriptions do not work for everyone. "Nobody is quite sure what to do with those wanting to quit, as this is all so new," says Ira Sachnoff, the president of Peer Resource Training and Consulting in San Francisco, which trains students to educate their peers about smoking and vaping. "We are all searching for quit ideas and services for this new nicotine delivery method. It is desperately needed."[64] In the meantime, researchers hope that long-term studies on vaping will eventually help them develop effective protocols for quitting.

One Family's Experience

Because little is known about the most effective way to overcome e-cigarette addictions, families are left on their own to figure out what works. The Debono family of Bloomfield Hills, Michigan, has struggled to help their three teens quit vaping. At first, Pam Debono thought vaping was just a phase. Like many trends, she assumed it would become old and her three teenagers would move on to something new. She also did not realize the tight grip that vaping had on her children, ages seventeen through twenty. "At first we thought, 'It's just a phase that takes wanting to quit, some self-discipline, and then it's done,'"[65] Debono says. She and her husband tried the usual parenting methods when they caught their kids vaping, such as grounding them or cutting off their allowance so they did not have money to buy nicotine pods. Nothing worked.

> "The science of vaping cessation hasn't caught up with the tremendous rise in use. There really isn't much out there that's been proven."[66]
>
> —Linda Richter, director of policy research and analysis at the Center on Addiction

Eventually, the Debonos acknowledged the hold that vaping had on their children. They tried NRTs such as nicotine patches and gum, but they experienced little success. As they tried to quit, the teens suffered common withdrawal symptoms, including disrupted sleep, anxiety, and moodiness. Even when the teens managed to stop vaping, stress often triggered them to start again as a way to calm down and relax. Now, Debono has resorted to giving her children random nicotine tests via home testing kits, hoping this will prevent them from vaping.

Searching for Solutions

Medical professionals are struggling to treat those addicted to vaping because there is little data on what methods actually work. Linda Richter, the director of policy research and analysis at the Center on Addiction, says that the lack of tested or approved methods for quitting e-cigarettes is a problem for the growing number of people addicted. "The science of vaping cessation hasn't caught up with the tremendous rise in use," Richter says. "There really isn't much out there that's been proven."[66]

In response, the FDA held a public hearing in January 2019 to discuss ways to help young people addicted to nicotine stop using e-cigarettes. Among the methods discussed were drug therapies that might help teens combat e-cigarette addiction. However, some professionals warn that more research is needed before young vapers are given medication and other powerful substances, even those intended as treatment. "We can't say just because you are vaping e-cigarettes, 'I am going to give you a nicotine patch or nicotine gum,' because we don't really know how addicted these kids are to the nicotine in e-cigarettes," says Suchitra Krishnan-Sarin, a professor of psychiatry at the Yale University School of Medicine. "We need to understand that first before we move to the medication realm."[67]

Another idea discussed at the FDA hearing was using technology embraced by teens to help them break the vaping habit. To this end, the Truth Initiative, a nonprofit organization known for its antismoking ads targeting young people, has created an innovative text messaging program to help youth quit vaping. The program allows anyone to text "QUIT" to a hotline (202-804-9884), free of charge and anonymously. After choosing their age bracket, users receive daily text messages of support and tips for quitting that are tailored to them. When designing the program, the group worked with young people who had already quit e-cigarettes and were in the process of quitting to make their messages more effective.

> "We can't say just because you are vaping e-cigarettes, 'I am going to give you a nicotine patch or nicotine gum,' because we don't really know how addicted these kids are to the nicotine in e-cigarettes."[67]
>
> —Suchitra Krishnan-Sarin, a professor of psychiatry at the Yale University School of Medicine

Students at Woodrow Wilson High School in Washington, DC, were some of the first in the country to try the text-based vaping cessation program. The school's students have a unique phone number so Truth Initiative researchers can analyze how the program performs at the school. Principal Kimberly Martin plans to blast information about the program to her school community to get as many people involved as possible. Anya, a senior at Wilson High, regularly uses e-cigarettes and is thinking about en-

Supporters of the Truth Initiative conduct a protest. The organization, which strives to turn youth away from tobacco and vaping, has developed a unique text-messaging program to help teens quit vaping.

rolling in the program. "I've always looked at the 'smoke to quit' ads on the metro and I've thought, 'That's a good idea.'"[68] Now she believes using the same type of text hotline for e-cigarettes can help many users who want to quit.

New Approaches Tailored to Youth

Across the country, local communities and organizations have stepped up to help people, especially youth, quit vaping. In Colorado, the minimum age for the Colorado QuitLine, a free service for Colorado residents to help them quit smoking, used to be fifteen. Given the skyrocketing rates of teen vaping, however, the state's health department lowered the age so that youth as young as twelve can call for help. Callers can work with a coach over the phone to understand what triggers them to vape, learn ways to manage cravings, and deal with relapse. "Kids as young as middle school are using these devices at alarming numbers so we want to make sure they have evidence-based help to quit those products if they choose to,"[69] says Alison Reidmohr, a tobacco communication specialist with the Colorado Department of Public Health and Environment.

Perhaps the most important antivaping strategy is to give people accurate health information about vaping. "The perception adults and media give that e-cigarettes are harmless is a big part of our problem," says Valerie Phillips, a physical education teacher in Round Rock, Texas. "Kids don't understand what's in it; they think it's just flavored water vapor."[70] In response, the nonprofit organization CATCH My Breath provides middle and high schools a free curriculum to teach students what chemicals are present in vaping pods and how these can harm health. Students also learn about vaping marketing techniques and are taught strategies to avoid getting caught in the buzz around vaping. In her middle school, for example, Phillips has integrated four CATCH My Breath vaping lessons into physical education activities. In one lesson, students learn about the health effect of chemicals

Peer-to-Peer Education

Some schools are enlisting their own students in the fight against vaping. When harsh punishments and sophisticated vaping detectors in the school bathrooms did little to stop students from vaping, Gregg Wieczorek, the principal of Arrowhead High School in Milwaukee, Wisconsin, tried a new approach. He recruited high school students to go into the district's seven middle schools to talk to younger students about the dangers of vaping and the risk of becoming addicted. He hopes that if younger students see older students talking about the dangers of vaping, it might leave a deeper impression than what teachers and parents can give.

In other schools, students are creating antivaping campaigns for their school districts. In Charles County, Maryland, for example, students researched the health effects of vaping and created a series of public service announcements that were played over the morning announcements in the community's middle and high schools.

found in vaping e-liquids and participate in a relay race to name the different chemicals.

In Orange County, California, educators are using a social and emotional learning (SEL) approach to antivaping education. As part of the state's Tobacco Use Prevention Education (TUPE) program, the antivaping lessons help students develop SEL skills, such as self-regulation, problem solving, and communication. They learn to apply these skills in situations where they might feel pressure to vape. In addition to the SEL lessons, students also receive information about vaping, a hotline number for quitting, and student-led antismoking and antivaping projects in their school and community. "They're learning how to deal with social pressure, how to respond to family dynamics and stress," says Ryan Crowdis, the TUPE program manager for Orange County, which is currently running the program in eight area districts. "Any young person can learn from that kind of information."[71] If students are caught vaping at school, a TUPE-trained staff member talks to them about why they decided to vape so they can learn to make a better decision the next time.

No Quick Fix

Addiction experts caution that there is no quick fix for overcoming an addiction to e-cigarettes. What works for one person may not work for another. Users who are serious about quitting may need to try a combination of approaches before they find one that works. With effort, however, it is possible to beat the addiction. Armed with knowledge of the risks and problems e-cigarettes can cause, perhaps the best approach is to avoid the addiction entirely by not trying e-cigarettes in the first place.

Source Notes

Introduction: A New Epidemic

1. Quoted in Maggie Fox, "Surgeon General Calls for 'All Hands on Deck' to Fight Teen Vaping," NBC News, December 18, 2018. www.nbcnews.com.
2. Quoted in Fox, "Surgeon General Calls for 'All Hands on Deck' to Fight Teen Vaping."
3. Quoted in Angelica LaVito, "CDC Says Smoking Rates Fall to Record Low in US," CNBC, November 8, 2018. www.cnbc.com.
4. Quoted in "Results from 2018 National Youth Tobacco Survey Show Dramatic Increase in E-Cigarette Use Among Youth over Past Year," US Food & Drug Administration, November 15, 2018. www.fda.gov.
5. Quoted in Leah Campbell, "Juuling: The Addictive New Vaping Trend Teens Are Hiding," Healthline, August 17, 2018. www.healthline.com.

Chapter One: The Smoke-Free Addiction

6. Nick English, "I Started Vaping to Quit Smoking, and It Was a Huge Mistake," *Men's Health*, October 22, 2018. www.menshealth.com.
7. English, "I Started Vaping to Quit Smoking, and It Was a Huge Mistake."
8. English, "I Started Vaping to Quit Smoking, and It Was a Huge Mistake."
9. Quoted in Renata Birkenbuel, "The New Nicotine Addiction: US Teen Vaping Stats Spike in 2018," *Newsweek*, December 18, 2018. www.newsweek.com.
10. Quoted in Maggie Fox, "Is Teen Vaping Really an Epidemic? These Experts Say Yes," NBC News, September 15, 2018. www.nbcnews.com.

11. Quoted in Kari Paul, "Flavored Vapes Lure Teens into Smoking and Nicotine Addiction, Study Shows," MarketWatch, February 26, 2019. www.marketwatch.com.

12. Quoted in Marina Pitofsky, "Millions of Teens Are Vaping Every Day. Here's What They Have to Say About the Trend," *USA Today*, December 20, 2018. www.usatoday.com.

13. Quoted in Tammy La Gorce, "The Vaping Epidemic That's Fogging Up NJ Schools," *New Jersey Monthly*, September 10, 2018. https://njmonthly.com.

14. Quoted in La Gorce, "The Vaping Epidemic That's Fogging Up NJ Schools."

15. Quoted in Pitofsky, "Millions of Teens Are Vaping Every Day."

16. Quoted in Pitofsky, "Millions of Teens Are Vaping Every Day."

17. JUUL, home page. www.juul.com.

18. Quoted in Gigen Mammoser, "Chemicals Used in E-Cig Flavors Are Toxic and We've Known for Decades," Healthline, November 15, 2018. www.healthline.com.

19. Quoted in Mammoser, "Chemicals Used in E-Cig Flavors Are Toxic and We've Known for Decades."

20. Quoted in Campbell, "Juuling."

21. Quoted in Dennis Thompson, "Many Young Juul Users May Not Know They're Addicted," HealthDay, October 19, 2018. https://consumer.healthday.com.

22. Quoted in Thompson, "Many Young Juul Users May Not Know They're Addicted."

Chapter Two: Why Are E-Cigarettes and Vaping So Addictive?

23. Richard Stumacher, "Pod Mods and Vaping Are Creating a New Generation of Youths Addicted to Nicotine," Stat News, September 21, 2018. www.statnews.com.

24. Quoted in Annette Meza, "Vaping Is a Big Trend Among College Students," Crusader News, October 31, 2018. https://crusadernews.com.

25. Quoted in Jennifer Fuentes-Tamu, "Does Vaping Prep Teens for Lifelong Addiction?," Futurity.org, August 25, 2015. www.futurity.org.

26. Quoted in "Study: Juuls Have Similar Nicotine Level as Cigarettes, Absorbed by Body Faster," UPI, September 12, 2018. www.upi.com.

27. Nora Volkow, "Recent Research Sheds New Light on Why Nicotine Is So Addictive," *Observations* (blog), *Scientific American*, September 28, 2018. https://blogs.scientific american.com.

28. Quoted in Caroline Kee, "18 People Talk About What It's Like Trying to Quit the Juul," BuzzFeed News, January 9, 2019. www.buzzfeednews.com.

29. Quoted in Nancy A. Melville, "Nicotine's Highly Addictive Impact on Youth Underestimated," Medscape.com, January 3, 2017. www.medscape.com.

30. Quoted in Zen Vuong, "Teens Who Vape Higher Doses of Nicotine Are More Likely to Become Regular Smokers," USC News, October 23, 2017. https://news.usc.edu.

Chapter Three: How People Become Addicted to E-Cigarettes and Vaping

31. Quoted in Justin Gray, "More Teens Are Vaping Regularly According to New Survey," WSBTV.com, December 17, 2018. www.wsbtv.com.

32. Quoted in Jan Hoffman, "The Price of Cool: A Teenager, a Juul, and a Nicotine Addiction," *New York Times*, November 16, 2018. www.nytimes.com.

33. Quoted in Hoffman, "The Price of Cool."

34. Quoted in Hoffman, "The Price of Cool."

35. Quoted in Hoffman, "The Price of Cool."

36. Quoted in Diane Moca, "Vaping a Growing Fad for Teens Who Think It's Safe, Officials Tell Naperville Commission," *Chicago Tribune*, April 13, 2018. www.chicagotribune.com.

37. Quoted in Della Hasselle, "Overcoming the Impulse: How a Teen Vaping 'Epidemic' Is Playing Out in Louisiana," *New Orleans Advocate*, December 22, 2018. www.theadvocate.com.

38. Quoted in Hasselle, "Overcoming the Impulse."

39. Quoted in Laura Kelly, "Teens Dabbling with E-Cigarettes Blindsided by Nicotine Addiction," *Washington Times,* January 7, 2019. www.washingtontimes.com.

40. Quoted in Kelly, "Teens Dabbling with E-Cigarettes Blindsided by Nicotine Addiction."

41. Juul, home page. www.juul.com.

42. Quoted in Rachel Becker, "Why Is Juul Worth $16 Billion? It's More Like a Cigarette than You Think," The Verge, July 3, 2018. www.theverge.com.

43. Martha de Lacey, "Why I Wish I'd Never Taken Up Vaping," *Sunday Telegraph* (London), March 1, 2015. www.telegraph.co.uk.

44. Quoted in *Here & Now,* "Vaping's Popularity—Especially Among Teens—Is Cause for Concern, Researcher Says," WBUR, May 16, 2018. www.wbur.org.

45. Quoted in Scott Maier, "Trying to Quit Smoking? E-Cigarettes Add Health Risks Rather than Help," University of California, San Francisco, July 30, 2018. www.ucsf.edu.

46. Quoted in John Sharp, "'Addicted for Life': A Surge of Vaping Among Teens Alarms Alabama," AL.com, December 23, 2018. www.al.com.

Chapter Four: Affecting Lives

47. Quoted in Moca, "Vaping a Growing Fad for Teens Who Think It's Safe, Officials Tell Naperville Commission."

48. Quoted in John Daley, "He Started Vaping as a Teen and Now Says Habit Is 'Impossible to Let Go,'" *All Things Considered,* National Public Radio, June 7, 2018. www.npr.org.

49. Quoted in Daley, "He Started Vaping as a Teen and Now Says Habit Is 'Impossible to Let Go."

50. Quoted in University of Rochester Medical Center, "First-Ever Study Shows E-Cigarettes Cause Damage to Gum Tissue," November 16, 2016. www.urmc.rochester.edu.

51. Quoted in University of Rochester Medical Center, "First-Ever Study Shows E-cigarettes Cause Damage to Gum Tissue."

52. Quoted in Susan Scutti, "Teen Develops 'Wet Lung' After Vaping for Just 3 Weeks," CNN, May 17, 2018. www.cnn.com.

53. Quoted in Kate Zernike, "'I Can't Stop': Schools Struggle with Vaping Explosion," *New York Times,* April 2, 2018. www.ny times.com.

54. Quoted in *USA Today* High School Sports, "Father Sues School After Son Suspended from Football Team for Having Vape Pen," October 27, 2017. https://usatodayhss.com.

55. Ahmed Kabil, "Confessions of a Juul Junkie," Medium, December 4, 2018. https://medium.com.

56. Kabil, "Confessions of a Juul Junkie."

57. Kabil, "Confessions of a Juul Junkie."

58. Quoted in Maggie Fox and Lauren Dunn, "Vaping First Sent This Teen to the ER, Then into Rehab," *Today*, January 18, 2019. www.today.com.

59. Quoted in Fox and Dunn, "Vaping First Sent This Teen to the ER, Then into Rehab."

60. Quoted in Maggie Lager, "Interview with a 15 Year Old Juul Addict," Knight Life, May 17, 2017. https://knightlifenews.com.

Chapter Five: Overcoming E-Cigarette and Vaping Addiction

61. Quoted in Jayne O'Donnell, "Depression, Anxiety, Nicotine Withdrawal: Trying to Quit Vaping 'Was Hell.'" *USA Today*, December 27, 2018. www.usatoday.com.

62. Quoted in O'Donnell, "Depression, Anxiety, Nicotine Withdrawal."

63. Maxwell Zeff, "Clearing the Air: Confessions of a Former Juul Addict," *Daily Collegian*, October 23, 2018. https://daily collegian.com.

64. Quoted in Jan Hoffman, "Addicted to Vaped Nicotine, Teen-agers Have No Clear Path to Quitting," *New York Times*, December 18, 2018. www.nytimes.com.
65. Quoted in Hoffman, "Addicted to Vaped Nicotine, Teenagers Have No Clear Path to Quitting."
66. Quoted in Dennis Thompson, "As Millions of Teens Get Hooked on Vaping, What Works to Help Them Quit?," HealthDay, January 31, 2019. https://consumer.healthday.com.
67. Quoted in Cynthia McFadden and Kenzi Abou-Sabe, "New Program Launched to Help Curb Teen Vaping Epidemic," NBC News.com, January 18, 2019. www.nbcnews.com.
68. Quoted in McFadden and Abou-Sabe, "New Program Launched to Help Curb Teen Vaping Epidemic."
69. Quoted in Jim Hooley, "Age Eligibility for Colorado QuitLine Lowered as Vaping, Smoking Increases," KDVR, November 14, 2018. https://kdvr.com.
70. Quoted in Holly Korbey, "Schools Respond to the Rise of Student Vaping," Edutopia, June 29, 2018. www.edutopia.org.
71. Quoted in Korbey, "Schools Respond to the Rise of Student Vaping."

Center on Addiction
633 Third Ave., 19th Fl.
New York, NY 10017-6706
website: www.centeronaddiction.org

The Center on Addiction is a nonprofit organization dedicated to helping people address addiction. Its website has information about addiction, prevention, and treatment for a variety of substances, including e-cigarettes.

National Institute on Drug Abuse (NIDA)
6001 Executive Blvd., Room 5213
Bethesda, MD 20892-9561
website: www.drugabuse.gov

Part of the National Institutes of Health, NIDA supports research efforts that improve drug abuse prevention, treatment, and policy. Its website links to the NIDA for Teens site, which is designed especially for young people and provides a wealth of information about various drugs, including nicotine and e-cigarettes.

Nicotine Anonymous
6333 E. Mockingbird Ln., Suite 147-817
Dallas, TX 75214
website: https://nicotine-anonymous.org

Nicotine Anonymous is a nonprofit twelve-step program for people seeking to live nicotine-free lives. Its website provides information about meetings and events, a newsletter, and other information.

Office of the Surgeon General
200 Independence Ave. SW, Suite 701H
Washington, DC 20201
website: www.surgeongeneral.gov

The Office of the Surgeon General provides Americans with the latest scientific information available on how to improve their health and reduce the risk of illness and injury. Its website has information, news, and reports about smoking and vaping.

Truth Initiative
900 G St. NW, 4th Fl.
Washington, DC 20001
website: www.truthinitiative.org

The Truth Initiative is a nonprofit public health organization dedicated to reducing tobacco use. Its website has information, policy studies, and research about tobacco and e-cigarettes.

US Food and Drug Administration (FDA)
10903 New Hampshire Ave.
Silver Spring, MD 20993
website: www.fda.gov

The FDA is the federal agency responsible for protecting and promoting public health through the control and supervision of food safety, tobacco products, and more. The FDA website has information, news, and research about tobacco products, including e-cigarettes.

Books

Elissa Bass, *E-Cigarettes: The Risks of Addictive Nicotine and Toxic Chemicals*. New York: Cavendish Square, 2016.

Kari A. Cornell, *E-Cigarettes and Their Dangers*. San Diego: BrightPoint, 2020.

Peggy J. Parks, *The Dangers of E-Cigarettes*. San Diego: ReferencePoint, 2017.

Christine Wilcox, *E-Cigarettes and Vaping*. San Diego: Reference-Point, 2016.

Internet Sources

Renata Birkenbuel, "The New Nicotine Addiction: US Teen Vaping Stats Spike in 2018," *Newsweek*, December 18, 2018. www.newsweek.com.

Centers for Disease Control and Prevention, "Electronic Cigarettes." www.cdc.gov.

MarketWatch, "Millions of Teens Are Addicted to Vaping, and There's Nothing Anyone Can Do About It," January 16, 2019. www.marketwatch.com.

Betsy McKay, "Teen Vaping Has Created Addicts with Few Treatment Options," *Wall Street Journal*, December 18, 2018. www.wsj.com.

National Institute on Drug Abuse, "Electronic Cigarettes." www.drugabuse.gov.

Michael Nedelman, "Why Vaping Is So Dangerous for Teens," CNN, January 17, 2019. www.cnn.com.

Office of the Surgeon General, "E-Cigarette Use Among Youth and Young Adults: A Report of the Surgeon General, Executive Summary," 2016. https://e-cigarettes.surgeongeneral.gov.

Index

Picture Credits

Cover: Thanakorn Hongphan/Shutterstock.com

6: Maury Aaseng

9: licsiren/iStockphoto.com

13: info.cineberg.com/Depositphotos.com

17: 6okean/iStockphoto.com

22: Maury Aaseng

25: steveheap/Depositphotos.com

27: diego_cervo/iStockphoto.com

32: R1im/Depositphotos.com

36: buenaventura/Shutterstock.com

40: hsyncoban/iStockphoto.com

44: mrfiza/Shutterstock.com

48: RossHelen/Shutterstock.com

51: fizkes/Shutterstock.com

54: Phat1978/Shutterstock.com

57: Eddie Jordan Photos/Shutterstock.com

60: AP Images for Truth Initiative

Carla Mooney is the author of many books for young adults and children. She lives in Pittsburgh, Pennsylvania, with her husband and three children, and she enjoys learning about issues that affect today's teens.